The Death of Conrad Unger: Some Conjectures Regarding Parasitosis and Associated Suicide Behavior

The Death of Conrad Unger:

Some Conjectures Regarding Parasitosis and Associated Suicide Behavior

Gary J. Shipley

dead letter office

BABEL Working Group

punctum books ✶ brooklyn, ny

THE DEATH OF CONRAD UNGER: SOME CONJECTURES REGARDING PARASITOSIS AND ASSOCIATED SUICIDE BEHAVIOR
© Gary J. Shipley, 2012.

This work is licensed under the Creative Commons Attribution-NonCommercial-NoDerivs 3.0 Unported License. To view a copy of this license, visit: http://creativecommons.org/licenses/by-nc-nd/3.0, or send a letter to Creative Commons, 444 Castro Street, Suite 900, Mountain View, California, 94041, USA.

This work is Open Access, which means that you are free to copy, distribute, display, and perform the work as long as you clearly attribute the work to the authors, that you do not use this work for commercial gain in any form whatsoever, and that you in no way alter, transform, or build upon the work outside of its normal use in academic scholarship without express permission of the author and the publisher of this volume. For any reuse or distribution, you must make clear to others the license terms of this work.

First published in 2012 by
dead letter office, an imprint of punctum books
BABEL Working Group
Brooklyn, New York

The BABEL Working Group is a collective and desiring-assemblage of scholar-gypsies with no leaders or followers, no top and no bottom, and only a middle. BABEL roams and stalks the ruins of the post-historical university as a multiplicity, a pack, looking for other roaming packs and multiplicities with which to cohabit and build temporary shelters for intellectual vagabonds (www.babel workinggroup.org).

ISBN-13: 978-0615600307

Library of Congress Cataloging-in-Publication Data is available from the Library of Congress.

for Conrad

Table of Contents

I. Introduction

II. Parasitoidal Possession

III. Four Literary *felos de se*: Nerval, Wallace, Quin, and Woolf

IV(a). Conrad Unger: Snapshots of a Suicide

IV(b). Conrad Unger: Excerpts and Synopses

IV(c). Conrad Unger: Selected Underscorings and Marginalia

V. Conclusion

The Death of Conrad Unger: Some Conjectures Regarding Parasitosis and Associated Suicide Behavior

Gary J. Shipley

A book is a postponed suicide.

—Cioran

I. Introduction

There are ways of dying that don't involve death, and you can suffer them by the hour. These mechanisms of dying might more accurately be called protracted enervations, or infirmities of freedom. But these are cumbersome expressions, so I'll stick with dying. In instances of dead-life, a condition more prevalent than you might at first imagine, suicide is a method of undying, and this appears to be especially true of cases where the sufferer, the dead-lifer, is acutely aware of their own perished state. Many who have seen photographs of a suicide, or been unfortunate enough to have witnessed one firsthand, testify to the look of interrupted animation that is often present on the faces of these autogenous corpses: it is as if their ante-mortem emancipation were inscribed deep in the facial musculature, deep enough to leave the surface of the skin as a portrait of imperial governance. (Recall that most kissed of faces: *L' Inconnue de la Seine*.)

The recent death by suicide of my close friend,[1] Conrad Unger (writer, theorist, and amateur entomologist), caused me to confront not only the commonplaces of self-disposal, but also their connections to literary life and notions surrounding psychological possession, to revaluate in both fictional and entomological terms just what it is that drives someone like Unger to take his own life as a matter of course, as if it had always been his only rightful end.

---

[1] Conrad and I met at university in our late teens and remained friends up until his death. I was one of the last people he visited before embarking on his pre-suicide exile.

II. Parasitoidal Possession

The exalted suicides of some humans might appear to be completely antithetic to the suicide behaviors of insects parasitized by their entomopathogenic fungi or hairworms (*nematomorpha*). However, on closer inspection we begin to see how the manipulatory goals in the two cases can appear almost fused. But before delving into the possibility of parallels, let us first get clear about the parasitoidal process, as seen in ants infected by *Cordyceps unilateralis* and crickets/grasshoppers infected by hairworms.

Cordyceps unilateralis is an entomopathogenic fungi, particular to tropical forests, that is parasitic on ants. The spores of this parasitic fungus precipitate from suitably placed leaves and fix themselves to an ant's exoskeleton. Upon germinating they enter the ant's body through minute respiratory holes (spiracles) in the ant's tough cuticular armour. Once inside the ant, tiny mycelial filaments start to devour its non-essential tissues, while leaving vital organs intact. When the time comes to sporulate, the mycelia infiltrate the ant's brain, modifying its future discernment of pheromones. This chemical hijacking results in the infected ant scaling the stem of a plant and attaching itself to its apex, or to the underside of one of its leaves, by its mandibles. Destination reached, the fungus eats through the ant's brain, killing it in the process. The fungus continues to eat and grow until it is ready to reproduce, at which point its fruiting bodies bud from the ant's head and detonate, releasing a thick mist of airborne spores that drift down onto the forest floor and infect other ants.

Once the parasite is ensconced in its host, the host's fate is set, and its identity becomes that of the parasite. Labeling the ant's behavior, then, as in any way suicidal might appear fanciful, given that its identity is not its own but rather that of the parasite, for which the behavior represents the continuation of its lifecycle, and that the ant dies not from attaching itself to a leaf but from having its brain eaten. But this is to ignore two keys points: firstly, although the ant is subsumed by its host, it is still the demise of the ant that concerns us when investigating parities with human suicide; and secondly, that encephalophagia marks the ant's end is true only in a most literal sense, for its real end comes with displacement, when it isolates itself from its community, and it is this that marks what might be called the ant's suicide behavior.

The attribution of suicidal drives to arthropods is perhaps more clearly demonstrated in the case of hairworm infection. A hairworm's aquatic larva is ingested by a host insect, typically that of a terrestrial arthropod such as a cricket or grasshopper. While in juvenescence the miniscule hairworm nourishes itself on its host's internal tissues, slowly growing until it is somewhere between three and four times the length of its host. In order to continue its life cycle — living independently and reproducing — the adult hairworm must first find water. In order to achieve this next stage in its development the hairworm manipulates it's host's behavior, causing it to commit a nocturnal suicide by jumping into water, after which the adult worm swims free of its drowning vehicle and goes in search of a mate.

Hairworms are sometimes referred to as *Gordian worms*, due to the parasite's similarity to the knot fashioned by one-time peasant and Phrygian king Gordius. The knot came to symbolize a seemingly intractable problem, a cipher of such complexity that all attempts at solution appeared futile. Eventually in 333 B. C., after many had tried and failed, the knot was unfastened by Alexander the Great who, frustrated at finding no ends to facilitate an untying, used his sword to chop through the knot, thus producing the desired end post-solution. (An oracle had predicted that whoever could untie the knot would become king of Asia, a position Alexander went on to occupy, thereby fulfilling the prophecy.) What is important to note is how this "Alexandrian solution" mirrors the resolution that suicide affords to its perpetrator: like Alexander to the knot, a suicide responds to the labyrinthine perplexity of human life with an audacious and violent solution.[2]

III. Four Literary *felos de se:* Nerval, Wallace, Quin and Wolfe

When considering as our case studies various literary suicides by drowning or hanging, we find that the cause is often identified by the suicide as nothing more nefarious than the perpetual trial of routine, the dull uniformity of thought, the drab fug of human life itself, a condition to which death becomes ultimate remedy: one irrevocable act of annihilation replacing a necrotic inculcation of partial anni-

---

[2] Roman Emperor Gordian I was also a man of letters, his most well-known work being the long epic poem "Antonias." In common with both Gérard de Nerval and David Foster Wallace, he hung himself with his belt.

hilations. This suffocating dichotomy is evidenced in the work of Ann Quin, but perhaps nowhere more clearly than in this line from her last novel, *Tripticks*: "I know not what course others may take; but as for me give me liberty or give me death."[3] She opted for liberty (as *necro-autonomy*: death as a solution to the *external* thralldom) the following year. She was reported to have walked out to sea someway east of Brighton's Palace Pier, to be washed up west[4] next day in Shoreham Harbour. Quin, however, had been plagued by mental illness for most of her life, leading to hospitalization on a number of occasions. She had expressed a profound disquiet about "going over the edge" into full-blown psychosis, even preferring the monotony and ridiculousness of an existence made deliberately quotidian to such a perturbing and alienating alternative. Maybe, in light of this, it would be more accurate to single out the fear of future disruptions to human everydayness (autodeath as *necro-equipoise*: death as solution to an *internal* thralldom) as the most likely locus of Quin's suicidal urge, and even literary suicides in general. This latter diagnosis

---

[3] Ann Quin, *Tripticks* (Chicago: Dalkey Archive Press, 2002), 10.

[4] Thereby lending an eerie significance to a sentence from her first novel: "A man's body, presumably aged between fifty-five and sixty, has been found washed up on the beach on the west side of the pier" (Ann Quin, *Berg* [London: Paladin, 1989], 162).

receives further validation from Virginia Woolf, who stuffed her coat pockets with stones and slipped into the River Ouse, leaving amongst her final words the following testament of dread: "I begin to hear voices, and I can't concentrate. So I am doing what seems the best thing to do. [...] I can't fight any longer. [...] You see I can't even write this properly. I can't read."

On the strength of this it might appear that it is not so much the zombification of day-to-day living that drove these writers to their aqueous overcoming, but the inability (or feared inability) to ride out another fracturing of that very state. The answer, I suggest, is that neither is the primary cause (the parasitical entity), but rather both suggest that the problem lies with the suicide's conception of self. The anomaly arises through a process of radical disassociation: the victim gradually becomes un-able to unite their subjective and objective senses of self (how their identities are manifested to them internally, with how their identities are manifested to others, how they are manifested in the world). As a result of this fracturing they cannot substantiate the core of their identity in either their objective expositions of self or their subjective expositions of self, until eventually a terrifying and ultimately unendurable anonymity is achieved.[5]

David Foster Wallace's suicide by hanging in September 2008 was presaged by numerous references to necro-autonomy, as seen in excerpts from Wallace's last novel, *The Pale King*. In one such excerpt Lane Dean, a wiggler (or I.R.S. rote examiner), experiences the deadening effects of his work so acutely that his fantasies and daydreams are loaded with references to self-slaughter:

> Lane Dean summoned all his will and bore down and did three returns in a row, and began imagining different places to jump off of. [...] The beach now had solid cement instead of sand and the water was gray and barely moved, just quivered a little like Jell-O that's almost set. Unbidden came ways to kill himself with Jell-O.[6]

---

[5] That this voiding of self is inextricably linked with writing is a position that Maurice Blanchot helped advance: "what suits the work is perhaps that 'I' have no personality." This is inextricably tied to "the fundamental demand of the work." And again, quoting Keats: "the poet has [...] no identity." See Maurice Blanchot, *The Space of Literature* (Lincoln: University of Nebraska Press, 1989), 90, 180.

[6] David Foster Wallace, "Wiggle Room," *The New Yorker*, March 9, 2009: http://www.newyorker.com/

Dean even finds signs of earlier expirations, their processes invariably slow and inculcated, as when he learns that the former occupant of his Tingle had been sedulous to the extent of burning out the buzzer that hailed more work. But most striking of all is his next discovery: "Small strange identifications in rows on the blotter's front edge were, Lane Dean had realized, the prints of teeth that somebody had bent and pressed real carefully onto the blotter so that the indentations went way down and stayed there."[7] Picture the ant, his mandibles locked into that leaf's central vein. And now picture Lane Dean's predecessor repeatedly biting into his desk blotter, forcing his teeth down deep, marking his discontent in a trenched spoor of multiple deaths. The connection may at first appear tenuous, but both are succumbing to the destabilizing machinations of a parasitical entity, and the cordyceps' and the hairworm's corollary in Dean's predecessor's case is his *self* — or at the very least his idea of it, his idea of possessing an identity that is not necessarily represented by the activities of his everyday life. The biting is his vain attempt to make an indelible mark on his surroundings, to stamp his individuality on some part of the world. Of course on one level

---

fiction/features/2009/03/09/090309fi_fiction_wallace.

[7] Wallace, "Wiggle Room."

the vestigial evidence only serves to individuate him in terms of the uniqueness of the bite mark, but on another level this series of indentations reflects the exasperated motiva-tions of a perspectively singular self continually subjugated into a state of virtual irrelevance. In turn we will see how the perceived necessity (and ultimate impotence) of attempting to mark (or write) your way out of the thralldom of a perceived anonymity, if carried to the end, can only lead to a conclusion whereby the self is freed from that which frustrates its telos (that of indelibly distinguishing it from other versions of itself), i.e., the formulaic ubiquity of human life.

In a much-celebrated address, Wallace states:

> It is not the least bit coincidental that adults who commit suicide with firearms almost always shoot themselves in the head.[8] And the truth is that most of these suicides are actually dead long before they pull the trigger. And I submit that this what the real, no-bull value of your liberal-arts education is supposed to

---

[8] Recall how the decapitated head of Orpheus sang its way down the Hebrus and out to sea, and how it then lived out its bodiless life as a troglodytic oracle. The independent life of the head can also be seen in the methodology of modern cryogenics.

be about: How to keep from going through your comfortable, prosperous, respectable adult life dead, unconscious, a slave to your head[9] and to your natural default-setting of being uniquely, completely, imperially alone,[10] day in and day out.[11]

The problem being, as he goes on to remark, is that "It is unimaginably hard to do this, to stay conscious and alive, day in and day out."[12] Not only, then, does Wallace (along with Quin and Woolf) feel death in life that emanates from both internal and external sources of cerebral

---

[9] Blanchot on a letter to Rilke: "It is the low 'degree of consciousness' which puts the animal at an advantage by permitting it to enter into reality without having to be the center of it" (Blanchot, *The Space of Literature*, 135). Recall that young panther in the closing paragraph of Kafka's "A Fasting-Artist."

[10] "That had surely been the beginning, the separating of yourself from the world that no longer revolved around you, the awareness of becoming part of, merging into something else, no longer dependent upon anyone, a freedom that found its own reality": Ann Quin, *Berg* (London: Paladin, 1989), 153.

[11] David Foster Wallace, commencement speech given to the 2005 graduating class at Kenyon College: http://online.wsj.com/article/SB122178211966454607.html.

[12] Wallace [commencement speech].

automation, but also the inescapable realization that the supraconscious human state to which he alludes is at best fugacious, at worst a nebulous and despair-induced ganglion ill-equipped to stand up to any sustained analytic scrutiny. Gérard de Nerval even goes so far as to suggest that this experiential malaise, this feeling that one is somehow dead in life, is symptomatic of mental illness, a stance he illustrates at the close of "Aurélia," in which we get the following exchange,

> "Why," I asked, "do you refuse to eat and drink like everybody else?" "Because I'm dead," he replied. "I was buried in such and such a cemetery, in such and such a place...."[13]

Nerval goes on to speak of the inexplicability of such beliefs, and how they are connected to an illness that he himself was lucky to have evaded. Although one of the prime motivations behind his writing "Aurélia" was that of impressing Dr. Blanche, whose custody he was under in Passy, convincing him that he possessed a sober-mindedness and transparency that was, before treatment, sadly in

---

[13] Gérard de Nerval, *Selected Writings* (London: Penguin Classics, 1999), 316.

question,[14] it is nevertheless a revealing and intriguing illustration of how Nerval thought a healthy person would view the disaffected condition of the self-confessed animate corpse. Nerval tells of how this poor man inhabits a world of illusion, a world in which reality is distorted, in which truth and the possibility of a life of vigour and happiness are denied. That Nerval feels able, compelled even, to separate the two worlds so distinctly speaks of the devouring virulence of this "illusory" world from which he is now supposedly fugitive. He divides the two realms with an absolutism that emanates from fear and denial, creating a division that could not possibly sustain itself. For Nerval longed to escape not only the supervision of Dr. Blanche, but also his own "sickly fantasmagorias," those chimerical bugs that he felt were denying him authentic occupation of the real world. But ultimately he was unable to write himself out of Passy, or into some supraconscious connection with the real world — a connection that would disclose to him secrets with which to nourish his life; death was the nourishment he found.

---

[14] "Aurélia" was, as Richard Sieburth remarks, "strategically conceived by Nerval as a way of writing himself out of captivity": "Introductory Note," in Nerval, *Selected Writings*, 257.

But this is not the only way one can approach Wallace's suicide. For once again, as with Quin and Woolf, the details reveal the alternative diagnosis of necro-equipoise, with Wallace too having suffered mental health issues for most of his adult life; in his case, stultifying bouts of clinical depression. In the two years leading up to his death the depression had returned, and like Woolf he had found himself unable to write. This inability to write is crucial. For it is there, in the act of writing, that these suicides uncover the partial realization of a supra-conscious mode of existence and a temporary release from anonymity: the self — otherwise subordinated by everydayness, or by mental strictures, themselves engendered by the self being thwarted and weakened through prolonged contact with an everydayness to which it refuses to succumb — is instead transplanted into a series of textual artifacts peopled with characterological emblems of this necessary act of escapology. If his boredom is tantamount to "*soul-murdering,*" [15] then the all-consuming activity of multiplying perspectivites — self-breeding — can be seen as a rebirthing or distension of soul or self, a temporary solution to the paralyzing horror of anonymity (the work existing "like some collective anima figure whose permutations would at once be finite and

---

[15] Wallace, "Wiggle Room."

unlimited").[16] When this outlet is somehow exhausted, found to be wanting, or is denied to one of its dependents, then it is as if the vitality of life has already been removed, a partial death already enacted. That Woolf identified herself intimately with her work is evident from her personal correspondence; and during those times when her work was attacked, Woolf claimed to be sensible of the blows; more and more she felt she was the work, inseparable from it, that the work was the reality of her self and that without it she was rendered an obliterative absence, left nurturing the wraith-hollowed organ of a progressively itinerant and displaced identity.

Unlike the other cases considered here, Ann Quin's suicide had a witness. His name was Albert Fox. He was fishing from the beach and watched her initiate that fatal thalassic trudge. His account of the little he saw appeared in the local press. He is widely regarded as the last man to see her alive. But there was another man, a man named James Carroll, a Brighton-born entrepreneur reduced to vagrancy, and he watched her go under from the Palace Pier. His press statement was never printed; it was thought to be nothing more than the hallucinatory babble of a mouldering alcoholic. Carroll may have been on his uppers at the

---

[16] Nerval, *Selected Writings*, 274.

time, but prior to his statement there had never been any reported instances of behavior that would indicate F10.5 [17] or beyond. Although often considered to be apocryphal, Carroll's statement is something that, now 30 years sober, he still stands by, frequently citing that day's extraordinary event as the reason behind his recovery. These are the words that undid his testimony:

> Her head was still above the water when it first appeared. I thought it must have been a piece of her clothing come loose, a belt perhaps. But then it was too long, and the way it moved in the water . . . I could see it was alive. She'd gone under at this point, but it continued to grow and shift beneath the surface of the water. Its shape, the way it moved, jerking and zig-zagging, was just like a giant eel — must have been 20 foot long.

I for one do not believe that this can be dismissed as the ramblings of some delusional soak. But whether he did actually behold the untwining of a serpentiform ghoul, that the suicide was indeed "inside her" as it was with Anne

---

[17] The F10 scale measures the mental damage caused by alcohol: *International Classification of Diseases*, World Health Organization: http://www.who.int/classifications/icd/en/.

Sexton and Sylvia Plath and that this was it leaving, its last witnessed act, is still very much a matter of conjecture.

The last "act" of the *Camponotus leonardi* ant infected with *Ophiocordyceps unilateralis* is to fuse itself to a sapling by clamping its mandibles into the vein of a leaf. This agglutination cum coalescence of tree and suicide is well-established: present in the suicide of Judas Iscariot in Aceldama (his body, as Augustine elaborated,[18] eventually dropping to the earth and rupturing like a piece of ripe fruit), in the corpse of Goethe's Werther buried in the roots of a linden tree, and again in Beckett's weeping willow so prominent in *Waiting for Godot,* to name but some. Evidencing his trademark economy, Beckett makes short work of uniting the small expirations of everyday with man's ultimate end, while also managing to allude to the reproductive potency of the suicide/hanged man's legacy, as exhibited in the following exchange:

> ESTRAGON: What about hanging ourselves?
>
> VLADIMIR: Hmm. It'd give us an erection!
>
> ESTRAGON: (highly excited). An erection!

---

[18] Thereby yoking the diverging accounts in the Gospel of Matthew and Acts.

> VLADIMIR: With all that follows. Where it falls mandrakes grow. That's why they shriek when you pull them up. Did you know that?
>
> ESTRAGON: Let's hang ourselves immediately![19]

The roots of the mandrake [20] are not only strangely anthropoidal in form, but are also thought to be imbued with magical properties, properties that can supposedly be harnessed in a narcotic blend prepared from its toxic root; and the myths surrounding the victim's terminal discharge are likewise manifold: from the hanged man's seed springs forth man as hypogeal poison, as intoxicant, a necromancer's forked dildo and genitor of promiscuous zombies (the soulless and loveless, a brood of witch-born Stavrogins).[21]

---

[19] Samuel Beckett, *Waiting for Godot* (London: Faber and Faber, 1973), 17.

[20] For a novelization of the myths surrounding the mandrake see Hanns Heinz Ewers' *Alraune*.

[21] William Burroughs frequently associates the hanged man with a continued life-force, "A Nigra hangs from a cotton wood in front of The Old Court House . . . whimpering women catch his sperm in vaginal teeth": *Naked Lunch* (London: Flamingo, 1993), 76. Also see William Burroughs, *The Soft Machine* (London: Flamingo, 1995), 63.

Although, perhaps nowhere is this alliance of tree and suicide presented more literally than in Dante's *The Wood of Suicides* (Canto XIII). Having torn a leaf from a tree under Virgil's instruction, Dante is immediately chastised by his arboreal victim, one Pier delle Vigne:

> And the trunk of it called out: "Why are you tearing at me?
>
> It grew a little dark with blood and said,
> Once again: "Why are you dismembering me?
> Have you no spirit of compassion?
>
> Once we were men, now we are stumps and shoots."[22]

Immured in "knotted wood" and fed on by Harpies, these suicides pay for their transgression, their act negating all future acts, with eternal paralysis, a dead-life of wooden anxiety, the very state from which our literary suicides seek deliverance.[23]

---

[22] Dante, *The Divine Comedy* (Oxford: Oxford University Press, 1998), 98.

[23] Trees, suicide, and issues of freedom have been juxtaposed quite brilliantly by Daniel Dennett: "I can never decide whether this is a tragic or comic vision: the deterministic world unfolds over the eons, eventually producing creatures who gradually grow

There are many other instances of adaptive parasite manipulation, but one that is particularly relevant here is the phenomenon of giant gliding ants (*Cephalotes atratus*) feeding on bird droppings. These ants ingest the bird droppings and thereby ingest the nematode parasites contained within them, whose eggs then cause the host ant's gaster to become red and distended, so coming to resemble certain berries that are favoured by local birds. The birds then consume the berry-like ants and, of course, the parasites to which the ants are host, and so the cycle continues. Here we see, in its most blatant form, how the parasite transforms its host into a consumable product. Unger, for one, felt that his utterly compulsive and all-consuming writing habits had transformed him into a consumable (readable) product, that he had not so much produced consumable items, but was himself made consumable in them.

---

rationality and curiosity to the fatal point where they can be caused, inexorably, thanks to their very rationality, to see the futility of their frantic, scheming ways. And so they pass, in a final self-annihilating spasm of ratiocination, into complete stolidity. Perhaps that's what happened to trees! Perhaps in the olden days trees scampered about, preoccupied with their projects, until the terrible day when they saw the light and had to take root and 'vegetate'!": Daniel C. Dennett, *Elbow Room: The Varieties of Free Will Worth Wanting* (Oxford: Oxford University Press, 1984), 104.

If, as I have been suggesting, these writers do indeed incubate their suicides for many years — their lives being little more than displays of denial and nurture as the suicide grows and consumes them like feasting hairworms — then Nerval, aware of its presence but ignorant of its schedule, was leaving nothing to chance by carrying on his person for a number of years his ultimate means of dispatch: a grubby apron string for which he claimed an esteemed provenance. On the 26th of January, 1855 he finally put it to use, hanging himself in the rue de la Vieille-Lanterne.

"Nerval, it is said, wandered adrift in the streets before hanging himself. But aimless wandering is already death; it is the mortal error he must finally interrupt by immobilizing himself."[24] These words from Blanchot remind us of what it is that characterizes the cordyceps-infested ant as suicidal: the terminality of the untethered, the rootlessness of a suicide's final moments.

The suicide note left by Nerval for his aunt read as follows: "Do not wait up for me tonight, for the night will be black and white." This night, for Nerval, promised to be devoid of all the nebular uncertainties common to other nights; by promising to be one with the printed page,

---

[24] Blanchot, *The Space of Literature*, 102.

he foresees a night that will at last unite his literary output with his once ruptured and plague identity. Finally, after repeated proclamations about the illusion of his living death, a sickness to be overcome if one is to truly access the world, he makes it his own, or rather ceases to see himself as separate from it, and with this alliance comes the world, the reality that had seemed so distant and unreal.

The fruiting bodies that rupture the ant's head as they escape, the spores, the identities unleashed, represent the ripened fruit of an oblique death, a "little death, sour and green," a "borrowed, random death"[25] that comes from outside, imposed, alien and disowned. According to Blanchot, for a death to be sufficiently developed, appropriately mine, "It must be like my invisible form, my gesture, the silence of my most hidden secret." This is the death open to the literary suicide, for unlike their arthropodal counterparts (that are consumed rather than assimilated), their infestation not only becomes the truest picture of who they are, but they themselves find it becoming. But still there is work to be done, for "There is something I must do to accomplish it; indeed, everything remains for me to do: it must be my work. But this work is beyond me, it is that part of me upon which I shed no light, which I do not attain and of

---

[25] Blanchot, *The Space of Literature*, 126.

which I am not master."[26] The work of which Blanchot speaks is that of acceptance, wherein death becomes consonant with our sense of identity. But no light is shed, no attainment made and no mastery gained, because one does not go about shaping the end of self, rather one detects that it's that very end that has shaped them all along. This discovery is moonless and ungovernable; it is like realizing that you're in the process of being swallowed, and that it's only your foredoomed refusal to be food that prevents you from slipping down. The work is beyond he who undertakes it in the same way that a writer's work is beyond the writer: its terrain negates, and through negating embodies the very negation through which it was conceived, that haunted lacuna that originated it.

---

[26] Blanchot, *The Space of Literature*, 126.

IV(a). Conrad Unger: Snapshots of a Suicide

Conrad Unger's suicide on September 4, 2009, his 50th birthday, was considered inevitable, if not overdue, by those who knew him (as ineludible as Quin's, Woolf's, Wallace's or Nerval's), and yet when news of it reached us, his family and friends, we still saw need to question that sense of inevitability that we'd quietly absorbed so many years before and had lodged inside us ever since like some dull, gloomy dyspepsia. The inescapable truth is that he had long ago, like two of his favourite literary characters, Kirilov and Stavrogin, been "eaten up by an idea."[27]

A month prior to his death, Unger left his wife of eleven years and his twelve-year old daughter and took up residence in a studio flat approximately 40 miles from the family home. During his time there he had virtually no contact with the outside world: there were no callers, no telephone conversations, and no reported interaction with his neighbours. The only person he

---

[27] Fyodor Dostoyevsky, *The Devils* (New York: Penguin Books, 1971), 611.

is known to have spoken to during those four weeks was the proprietor of a local mini-mart, dialogues all of which were entirely utilitarian.

When I saw the photographs and the video footage of him hanging from that tree — five different people made and disseminated such documentation — I had trouble recognizing him. Maybe I hadn't wanted to recognize him. Or maybe I never had. The first photograph I saw was taken from some twenty or so metres away; he looked like a forlorn bug. Even in close-up this effect was not entirely lost: once gangling in his youth, his sedentary life-style had gifted him a marked tumescence around the midriff, while his arms and legs, though of more than sufficient length, had remained exceptionally thin for the appendages of a fully-grown man.

Unger was seen two days prior to his death, in a park across the street from his new lodgings, staring up at the branches of a large oak for more than an hour. His demeanour on that day is said to have been one of calm focus, bordering on serenity.

Unger spent the eve of his suicide eating a copy of every story and every novel he'd ever published. He kept his throat wet with brandy and marked every fifty pages with a slice of ripe pear.

A suicide note was discovered in his left trouser pocket: an adaptation of Father Time's departing scrawl in Thomas Hardy's *Jude the Obscure*, it read: "Done because I am too menny."

His was not the early to bed of Pessoa's Baron of Teive, his contagion torched in a fit of reason, but the full awakening of once fragmentary voices, their humble residue sliding down his inside leg, his day made black and white.

IV(b). Conrad Unger: Excerpts and Synopses[28]

Mirror-Blind (Novella, 1992): a reworking of the vampire myth in which the protagonist, Adrienne, kills just so that she can view her reflection.

"It's more than vanity: I have to be able to see the owner of all this. I have to witness that place of origin. Photographs do not only smile when I smile. And even though my reflection

---

[28] All the page numbers listed in this section are to first editions.

may be wet with murder, it is, however briefly, mine. Without it all my animations seem . . . hollow." (183)

In order to see himself, Unger exteriorized his internal states through writing. Adrienne, in order to see herself, is forced to ingest the interiors of others in repeated acts of destructtion. For Adrienne, the blood of others is quite literally the idiolect of self.

The Upturned Tree (Novel, 1996): a love story in which the jilted party commits suicide by planting himself in the ground head-first.[29]

"Staring down into the planting hollow, he caught sight of a worm he'd happened to bisect while digging. He watched as it quirked on the loose earth. Such is the violence of a nescient death, he thought, as he made root of his head, neck and upper torso, and waited for the soil to follow him down." (203)

The Lice Killers (Novel, 1999): this work features the braided stories of a collection of distinctly heterogeneous characters who all seek to alter the course of their lives in some way, but who

---

[29] Conrad confided in me on more than one occasion that entering into his daily life was not too far removed from the slow agonizing death heaped on this character.

all eventually end up doing and being what they'd hoped to avoid.

"When Mark thought about his children, grown up now and lost to him, he thought of them as ghosts, ghosts of tiny strangers that he'd made up and who had come and gone without him, leaving nothing to phantomize but their imagined imaginings of him, absent father-ghost. But Laura, Laura was different. Even before the weight of her body stretched the hemp Laura regretted nothing. She too had not managed to evade, but unlike the others had managed to assimilate that failure into a cumulative rearrangement of herself, eventually coming to embody the very impossibility of evasion." (161)

Seven Tales of Zero (Short Story Collection, 2005): A book of seven stories, only six of which were completed, unless you take the single sentence of the seventh as a tale in itself (which I do). As a story of a suicide's life it requires no further embellishment.

"Accepting that I was alive got progressively more difficult, but in time I was able to construct my future from it." (137)

IV(c). Conrad Unger: Selected Underscorings and Marginalia

Johan Nilsen Nagel (the hero of Knut Hamsun's *Mysteries*) carried a vial of prussic acid in his waistcoat pocket: "all he had to do was swallow it without grimacing too much." [30] (Text underlined in HB pencil.)

And later:

"The watch fell to the floor and he leaped out of bed. 'Someone is calling,' he whispered, and looked out the window with eyes bursting out of their sockets. [...] He reached the docks, ran to the farthest pier, and leaped into the sea. Some bubbles came up to the surface." [31] (Asterisks placed with HB pencil in the body of the text.)

The Horla, man's invisible replacement, became something of an obsession of Unger's; his numerous copies of both versions of Maupassant's

---

[30] Knut Hamsun, *Mysteries* (New York: Picador, 1976), 207.
[31] Hamsun, *Mysteries*, 253.

story are littered with underlining and marginalia:

"16 May. I am ill: that's certain! I have a fever, an atrocious fever, or rather a feverish weakness which afflicts my mind just as much as my body. All the time I have this terrible feeling of imminent danger, this apprehension of impending misfortune or approaching death, this presentiment which is doubtless the first sign of some disease, as yet unknown, germinating in my blood and my flesh."[32]

And later:

". . . he who shall die only at his appointed day, hour and minute, because he has reached the limit of his existence."[33] (Both sections of text circled in 2B pencil)

In the margin of Nerval's "Aurélia" beside the following line, "every man has a double and that when he sees him, death is near."[34] Unger had written, "I have seen the double inside and I must die." (Marginalia in HB pencil.)

---

[32] Guy de Maupassant, *Selected Short Stories* (London: Penguin Books, 1971), 315.
[33] Maupassant, *Selected Short Stories*, 344.
[34] Nerval, from "Golden Sayings," in *Selected Writings*, 270.

"a pure spirit buds beneath the husk of stones."[35] (Text circled in red biro.)

" 'A fuckin livin death, I tell you it's not being near alive, by the end I was undead, not alive, and I tell you the idea of dyin was nothing compared to the idea of livin like that for another five or ten years and only then dyin.' "[36] (Line ends struck through with yellow highlighter.) To the title, *Infinite Jest*, he'd added in black biro the words, "or coming to terms with suicide."

"I felt the crushing weight of evil insect control forcing my thoughts and feelings into pre-arranged moulds, squeezing my spirit in a soft invisible vice"[37] (Text struck though with yellow highlighter.)

"[...] death knows the way to my closet
he knows the way to my bedroom he knows how to get in my shoes
death knows how to tie knots in my fishing line
he unbuttons my shirts
he whets my knife death
like a rudder to the slaveship moon

---

[35] Nerval, *Selected Writings*, 374.
[36] David Foster Wallace, *Infinite Jest* (New York: Black Bay Books, 1997), 423.
[37] William Burroughs, *The Soft Machine* (Flamingo, 1995), 55.

with its sombre sarabandes like little footprints
like tombs put to music
songs that cannot be sung
listen how it tangles my tongue
and see here the spectators of death"[38]
(Crosses placed at the end of each line with HB pencil.)

"Crossing the bridge at that moment was a simply endless stream of traffic."[39]

And later:

"'because I've never been able to find the kind of nourishment I like. If I had found it, believe you me, I'd not have made this fuss but would have eaten my fill the same as you and everyone else.'"[40] (Text underlined in HB pencil, and then for the most part erased.)

"He spoke with an accent; I think he's a foreigner.

---

[38] Frank Stanford, *The Battlefield Where the Moon says I Love You* (Barrington, RI: Lost Roads Publishers, 2000), 118-19.

[39] Franz Kafka, "The Judgment," in *Franz Kafka Stories 1904-1924* (London: Abacus, 1981), 56.

[40] Franz Kafka, "A Fasting-Artist," in *Franz Kafka Stories*, 252.

He is. He came to this country some years ago. But he's here permanently now."[41] (Text bracketed in 2B pencil. Excessive indentation present.)

V. Conclusion

That fine mesh dream of self (that mycelial human curse) expands in the brain, bloating it with plans and coordinates, pasts and futures, its seemingly eternal patterns of redemption floating purposeful in the skull air like tiny filaments brushed from the brain of God. And then somewhere down the line my friend's uneven teeth clamped tight in the unseasonably hot sun. Back there in that park, his body hanging rigid in place, his brain finally devoured by the ravening dream, his ruptured skull eaten free of the rooted silos of concretized thought — the rope a tumoral stick cum fruiting alien limb cum stroma stretching its perverse destiny into the sweat air. With eyes filled with black smoke, and mouth seduced into an unholy seal of lipless teeth, he rained his dream on us.

---

[41] Jerzy Kosinski, *Steps* (New York: Random House, 1968), 62.

What is left for me to say?

Too much and so, in the end, nothing.

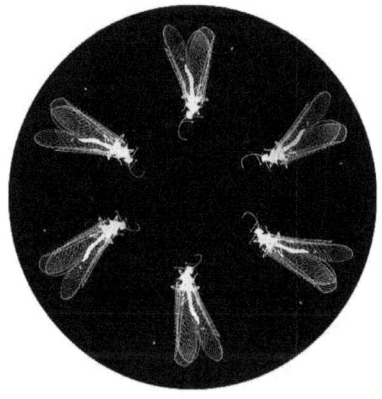

W. dreams, like Phaedrus, of an army of thinker-friends, thinker-lovers. He dreams of a thought-army, a thought-pack, which would storm the philosophical Houses of Parliament. He dreams of Tartars from the philosophical steppes, of thought-barbarians, thought-outsiders. What distances would shine in their eyes!

~Lars Iyer

www.babelworkinggroup.org

www.ingramcontent.com/pod-product-compliance
Lightning Source LLC
Chambersburg PA
CBHW070939180426
43192CB00039B/2385